Hearing

By Sharon Gordon

Consultants
Nanci R. Vargus, Ed.D.
Primary Multiage Teacher
Decatur Township Schools, Indianapolis, Indiana

Jan Jenner, Ph.D.

Children's Press®
A Division of Scholastic Inc.
New York   Toronto   London   Auckland   Sydney
Mexico City   New Delhi   Hong Kong
Danbury, Connecticut

Designer: Herman Adler Design
Photo Researcher: Caroline Anderson
The photo on the cover shows a young boy cupping his ear to hear better.

Library of Congress Cataloging-in-Publication Data

Gordon, Sharon.
    Hearing / by Sharon Gordon.
      p. cm. — (Rookie read-about health)
    Includes index.
    Summary: This simple introduction to the sense of hearing discusses
how, and what, we hear.
    ISBN 0-516-22289-9 (lib. bdg.)   0-516-25989-X (pbk.)
    1. Hearing—Juvenile literature. [1. Hearing. 2. Ear. 3. Senses and
sensation.] I. Title. II. Series.
QP462.2 .G67   2001
612.8'5—dc21

                                   00-057022

Listen! Do you hear that?

Hearing is one of the five senses. The other senses are seeing, touching, smelling, and tasting.

You hear with your ears.

You have one ear on each side of your head. This helps you hear things all around you.

Look in a mirror.

You can only see part
of your ear. That part
is called the outer ear.

9

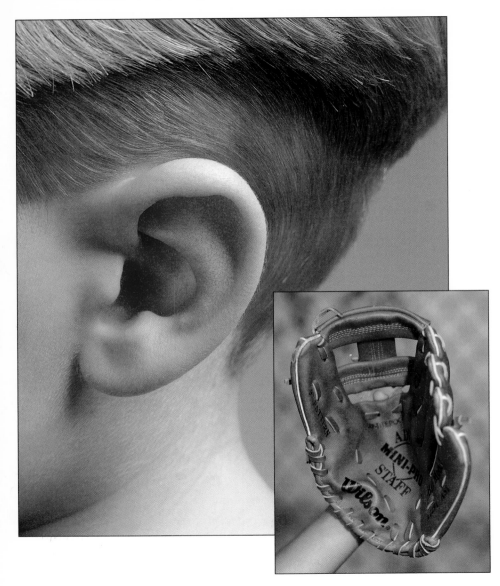

The outer ear is shaped like a baseball glove. It *catches* the sounds around you.

The sounds go into the little hole in your ear. They move through a tube into your middle ear.

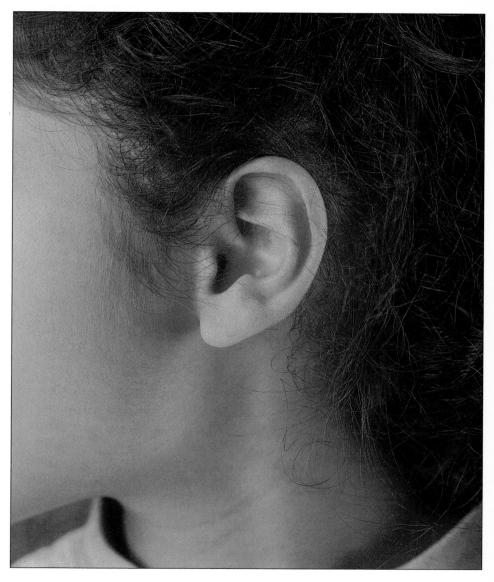

13

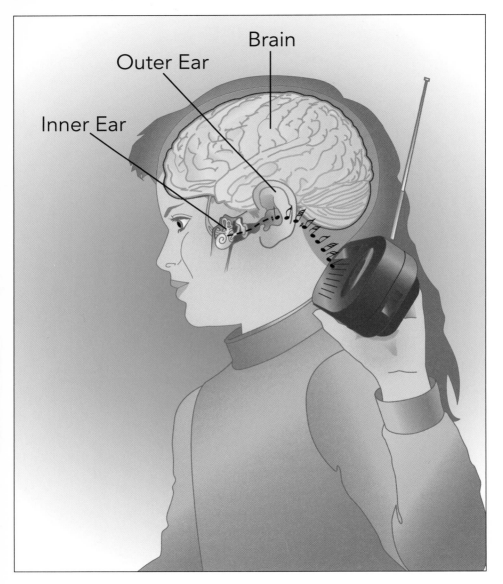

Brain

Outer Ear

Inner Ear

14

The sounds keep moving until they reach your inner ear. The inner ear sends them to your brain.

That is how you hear things.

If a sound is too soft, you can cup your hands around your ears to hear it better.

So that's what you heard!

You can cover your ears
if a sound is too loud.

Here comes the fire engine!

Some sounds make
you want to dance.

Others make you want
to clap your hands.

There are sounds that can wake you up.

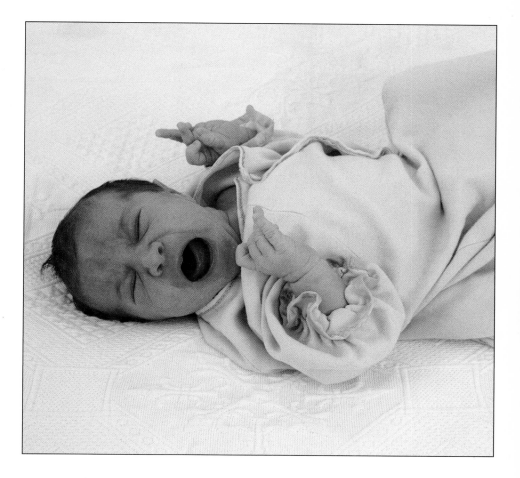

24

There are sounds that can put you to sleep.

Some sounds are high, like a whistle.

Some sounds are low,
like a drum.

And some sounds
are just plain fun.

Surprise!

Words You Know

baseball glove

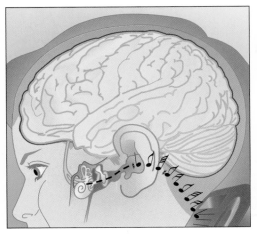

brain

drum

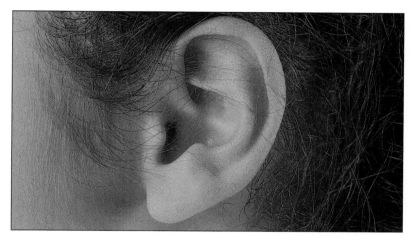

outer ear

sounds

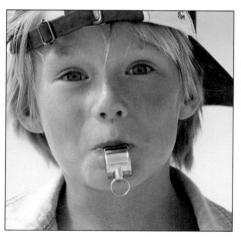

whistle

Index

About the Author

Sharon Gordon is a writer living in Midland Park, New Jersey. She and her husband have three school-aged children and a spoiled pooch. Together they enjoy visiting the Outer Banks of North Carolina as often as possible.

Photo Credits

Photographs ©: Corbis-Bettmann: 17, 31 bottom left (Brian Leng), 26, 31 bottom right (Wartenberg Picture Press), 24 (Doug Wilson); Mandy Rosenfeld: 18; Photo Researchers, NY: 10 left (Ken Cavanagh), 13, 31 top (Richard Hutchings); PhotoEdit: 3 (Gary Conner), 23 (Laura Dwight), 19 (Tony Freeman), 21, 27, 30 bottom right (Michael Newman), 16 (Mary Steinbacher), 20 (David Young-Wolff); Rigoberto Quinteros: 5, 6, 10 right, 30 top; Stone: 29 (Arthur Tilley); Visuals Unlimited: cover, 9 (Eric Anderson).

Illustration by Patricia Rasch.